Sonder: Poems of Healing & Connection

Sneha Christall

BookLeaf Publishing

India | USA | UK

Presentation by *BookLeaf Publishing*

Web: www.bookleafpub.com

E-mail: info@bookleafpub.com

ISBN:9789360948924

First edition 2024

DEDICATION

For,

My parents, who kept my dreams alive, when I couldn't...

ACKNOWLEDGEMENT

The world is a much better place thanks to people who see the good in others. Writing this book would not have been possible without the encouragement, support (and nudging) of my partner, Terrin.

I thank my sister, Priya who has been my 'forever sounding board'. Your humor and intelligence have largely contributed to my works in the editing stage.

I would like to thank my literature professors who helped shape my writing voice, and whose lessons I still go back to, when in doubt.

Lastly, thanks to all my friends who have taken the time to critique my work. Your perspective helps me write better.

PREFACE

The opportunity to write 'Sonder' came to me serendipitously when I came across BookLeaf Publishing's poetry writing challenge. However, the seeds of this book were laid much before. Some of the poems in this collection were written years prior. As a student of literature, I have taken time to hone my voice and work out what it is that I would really want to write about.

They say that to produce art, one must have suffered and have their heart broken. This holds true for me too. I believe that words hold the power of healing just as they do, harm.

Through this collection of poems, I explore different life experiences, in the hope that they are meaningful and offer support to you. So here I am, sharing with you my work of love.

Sonder

Far from the din of the city she called home —
with grey, smoke-choked skies, more people
than permissible per square foot, where history,
politics and commerce rubbed shoulders ever so
simply,
Her mind had been called to Stillness,
bewildering as it seemed.
Perhaps, it had something to do with—
The fleeting view of snow-clad mountains (mist
permitting), the sun's decidedly capricious
nature, the constant twitter of sparrows, the
sheer effort it took to walk uphill, the tea that
tasted so much more special (how?), or the lanky
trees that greeted her at every bend?
No wonder then, visitors from near and far,
found themselves extending their stay, some
going so far as to call this village their home.

. . . .

There was the long-haired, bearded,
bespectacled man, his most differentiating
feature being his uncanny height.
In his lap, snuggled a diminutive girl with bright
eyes and two nose rings. Her eyes darted across

the room to the young man playing a guitar and
the crowd surrounding him, but they always
came back to rest, to gaze upon her lover, as
they told each other sweet nothings —
The language that couples in the first flush of
love find most suitable for shutting others out,
much like a warm blanket on a chilly night.

……..

And then there was the fast-speaking American
woman with the tattoo of a phoenix all over her
back, a suitcase that could have easily fit two
small humans, toned arms and legs that gave
away her fitness penchant,
Who in the middle of a divorce, had decided that
she would backpack solo for the first time ever,
and discovered — quite serendipitously, an old
friend; learned that 'hostels' in India meant
'dorms' too, that she adored Kerala paratha, but
despised the lachha variety,
And that she was far braver than she gave
herself credit for.
At nighttime, as the hostel dog curled up against
her door, shivering silently, she found an old
jumper to shelter him in,
Soon after, she slept soundly.

……..

The next morning appeared, grey and rainy, and
in the space between night and day, walked a
woman in a crumpled blue raincoat. With long,
measured steps, she made her way to the
meditation retreat. A doctoral student from
Finland and a longtime student of Buddhism,
Her curt smile did little to give away her
anticipation of meeting the Dalai Lama later that
week.

……….

Atop a hillock overlooking the village below,
there sat a young man and his companion (for a
while), a furry black and white dog with an
animated tail. He (not the dog) took his time to
roll a joint and politely offering it to me, also
offered up his poetry.
A man who wrestled with numbers for a living,
quoted Hindi verses on life's apparent
ephemerality and held dreams of becoming a
grandfather with a lifetime's worth of memories,
Never staying too long in the same place,
making friends of everyone, yet bidding
goodbyes the next day,
Round the corner, he disappeared, the setting sun
behind him.

. . . .

Rationing time between her shifts to see more of
the mountains, was the girl who 'worked in IT',
but would much rather disappear and open up a
bakery in the woods.
Would she do it though?
Like the boy from Hyderabad, who quit his big
city job, set up shop next to the local grocer's,
where cows and goats grazed in the mornings,
And could be found, smoking a cigarette, till his
first customer appeared, hungry for some fresh
dosa, that he would prepare while watching
Suits on his mobile phone; a friendly sign above
the sink reading, "Help me by washing your
plate".
Like Mowgli, the 'jungle' had become his home.

. . . .

And then there was the young woman dressed in
a mish-mash of both Himalayan Hemp and
Nike, here to soak in her last few months in
India, before she left for the US,
Like a transient bird, she had nested here awhile
and now — was just "passing through".

………

All of 60 years, walking downhill while chatting
with ease, was the wildlife researcher, who much
preferred to live solitarily in the distant village
above (with birds and monkeys for company),
Till he didn't, so he could talk about why God
doesn't exist, about the virtues of staying
unmarried and why there's no creation more
beautiful than a woman.

………

Hands in his pockets, a thick shawl wrapped
around his neck and a glint in his eye, was the
writer on commission to complete his first work
of fiction, ready to offer guidance to this fellow
writer,
Who it appears, can describe others — strangers
even — in great detail, but is at a loss for words
when it comes to describing her own self.

………

Thank You

Leave your education, designation,
denomination,
Your bank balance and clout, at the gates
Where uniformed guards pat you down
Wordlessly, before you proceed.
Because, none of it matters once you find
yourself in the
Echoless chamber.

Up above, a lone ceiling fan
Creaks heavy with resignation,
Offering little respite to
The bodies huddled underneath,
Clamoring for space
On the slatted wooden benches.

In the great hall nearby, convened
Ordinary humans, tasked with the extraordinary.
Dressed in black garb, white collars,
And an all-important air,
They make a living out of blurring lines,
Molding the truth,
And finding the grey areas
That best suited their agenda.
As time wears on in the echoless chamber,

Exhaustion spills out in a hundred little ways.
While some guard themselves with masks and
sanitizer
And a phone to keep their hands busy,
Others' anger becomes pronounced by
Beating of chests, hurling of curses,
Howling, bawling cries,
Directed at the little old lady,
Dressed in black, seated above the rest,
A pedestal fan beside her.

She looks on in disinterest,
As a lesser mortal escorts
The now weeping individual out.
Another one would be here by tomorrow.

They are a motley crowd and yet,
None are here of their own accord.
Desperation is worn the same by everyone —
Sweat and tears intermingle,
As dreams built not so long ago,
By a younger, more hopeful version of
themselves,
Come crashing down,
Like a house built in haste,
On unsteady ground.
Now, no words remain to be said.

Thoughts, stifled by the monotonous call of

Names, numbers and years,
Are now indistinguishable, amidst
The slow humdrum of 'justice' being served —
A little here, some there,
A little delayed by another six months,
If you are lucky,
And a lot, by years,
If you aren't.

What is justice,
If not an attestation
To the human tendency to seek order
Amidst chaos,
Of trying to set things right,
As soon as they
Fall off?
Nearby,
In a little room tucked away,
Squeals and shouts of children
Fill the air.
Unaware of their parents' differences,
They play, finding friends
To build new games, rules,
Winners and losers.

There are no winners or losers
In the echoless chamber, however.

I sit in silence,

A song to calm me,
Its verses, steadying and centering me,
Reminding me of my own breath,
Which at times, had faltered,
But was yet to give up.
All this, for two minutes
With the little old lady,
Who had by now,
Retired to her AC room.

She hardly met my eye
As we bowed down.
And, with a single flourish of her pen,
Granted me my modicum of justice,
My own patch of blue sky,
That had colored my dreams vividly,
For over a year now.

Outside the echoless chamber,
Time sped on, like it always does.
A light afternoon breeze
Played with my hair,
As I found myself smiling,
Saying the same words
Over and over again —
Thank you,
Thank you,
Thank you…

Note:

This poem is an attempt to defamiliarize my experience with the Indian
court system during my divorce proceedings. It is interesting to add another
dimension to our experiences using this literary technique, and watch as readers come up with their own assumptions.

In the Bazaars of Agra

Round and round we go,
Through meandering alleys,
Each more similar than the next.
Unbothered by the rabble
Of hawkers, street dwellers and tourists
(Getting ripped off while thinking they snagged
a good deal),
Our rickshaw driver pulls to a stop:

'Have we arrived right where we started?'
There was no way of knowing for certain.
Back into the din we proceed,
The sun now scrutinizing us intently,
As shopkeepers, their clothes, bangles, spices,
mirrors and
Flowers (for weddings/ funerals, as fate
decides),
Clamor for our attention.

Far from the place we call home,
Our senses jolted by unfamiliarity,
Sights, sounds and smells collide,
Into one steady commotion.

Swallowed up whole, we realize —

Years of city-dwelling have rendered us
Tone-deaf to how
Life has the capacity to
Birth itself everyday.

In a few more days, we would leave
And in a few more years,
This would be a distant memory.

But the lesson remains —
We are mere passers-by,
With more in common
Than we are made to believe.
And if we ask of it without fear,
The vast ocean of life
Will keep on giving.

Note:

In this poem, I've tried to capture both an inner
and outer journey. The outer journey is that of
being in the Kinari Bazaar of Agra ('kinari'
translates to 'hem' in English. This meaning is
interesting because the actual bazaar seems to
have no end or 'hem', but is a perpetual maze of
circles, with no apparent beginning or end). The
inner journey is that of experiencing being the
'other' albeit, for a short time.

The structure of this bazaar acts as an allegory for the circle of life, an infinite continuum that keeps on giving to those who ask of it. Some more instances where this idea is reiterated is when we disembark from the rickshaw and are not sure if we have ended up right where we began, and the reference to both weddings and funerals. While one symbolizes new beginnings, the other marks the end of a life.

(Un)Guarded

Our dreams expose us for who we really are.
We spend our waking hours, spinning words that
bely our truth,
Inhabiting a hundred different bodies,
But the one we've been given.
We dare not see the others
Just like us, with stories waiting to be
Seen. Heard. Spoken for.

We spend a lifetime beholding them as
Strangers,
A lifetime, building Walls…
We dare not reach out and touch that fragile
thread
Of our shared irrational fears, bandaged hearts,
and hopes —
Despite it all.

Surely, our dreams are less confusing than
The reality we spin for ourselves.
In our dreams, our pain is more easily held.
We come undone
At a kind word, a connection that tells us
We are not alone,

And almost at once —
We become unguarded,
Honoring old wounds with scars
That whisper…
"You've made it this far",
"You are stronger than you realize",
"There are others, who in this very moment, feel
just as you do".

And so,
The pain we bear, becomes
A much lighter thing,
A sacred space,
Where we are seen as though, anew.

Don't you think that we long for the same,
simple things?
A hand that reaches out
And assures us,
That we needn't hush our hopes,
We can sing them out loud,
Knowing that more will join us,
And discovering in that moment of abandon,
that—

We are no longer dreaming,
But set awake,
Our eyes opened
To a new shore.

This Mat of Mine

This mat of mine,
Tapered at the edges now,
Sweat-stained in places,
Bearing impressions of my soles,
Has witnessed my surrender,
(Or attempt),
To pain, discomfort,
All that we spend
Our waking hours,
Trying to escape…

On this mat,
I have had many visitors—
Joy, a sudden gloom,
Vexation, delight,
I invite them in and
Celebrate their arrival,
Because they have been
Sent by the all-knowing.

Quiet calls to quiet,
Each breath, an arrival,
The teacher becomes
The student.

My heart opens up,
Reflecting on
My fellow companions
Who share this
Brilliant, evanescent,
All-consuming thing
We call 'life'.

My body now wilfully bending
Making space,
New shoots find their way
Through the mud,
It is morning somewhere,
As the birds sing its welcome,
There is space now to
Hold each other,
Look into another's eyes,
Know that
We have more in common
Than we are made to believe,

And that true, lasting happiness
Can be found on
A worn-out yoga mat.

l.o.v.e

In the beginning, love was simple,
One syllable and four letters,
To protect and disarm,
Build and renew.
Coupled with play and laughter,
Love picked you up when you fell,
Changed the way you saw yourself —
Most favored in your little kingdom,
Everything you desired seemed within reach.

And so you set out
Into a world waiting to be explored,
Each day, an adventure.
Not long after, you experience
Your first crush.
Nothing prepared you
For the surge of emotions
You now felt in your chest,
(Or more accurately,
The pit of your stomach).
This was love for
The very idea of love,
And you encountered it
With an innocence
That would soon wash away,

With experience in its wake.

Love can hurt,
When it confuses itself for
Pride, fear, jealousy…
You burn your fingers,
Learn to say "it's complicated",
Laugh as though you have never been hurt,
Losing parts of yourself,
And searching for them
In all the wrong places.

Love,
You collected it in bits and pieces
Everywhere you went,
But it was never enough,
Soon, you turn a corner,
You realize –
"Love, it always began with yourself".

And when it arrives again,
Love comes unannounced,
There is little you do
But give in to this familiar feeling,
And make space in your heart again
To hold another.

You do not remember the exact moment
"I" became "we",

You dream in color now,
And pray you do not lose
This thing that has become
So precious to you,

You are in the risky business of
Beginning to care again.

Trouvaille

(n.)
A chance encounter with something wonderful

Do you remember the exact minute
The song of your life changed?
You turn a corner,
And you have a reason to

Laugh a little louder,
Smile at passing strangers,
Notice the beam of sunlight
That has chosen to fall on your face,
Flowers by the wayside,
A burst of color,
Sweetly declaring
Their presence.

Here is a song in your heart,
And you know
Not to question it…

Blindingness

He emerged from his home,
Fully formed and morose looking,
A newborn unwilling to experience
Anything besides the dark inner lining of his
chrysalis.
It was with a certain disdain
That he regarded the world.

However, twisting out of his home,
He realigned,
Readjusted
To this strange new form of existence.
In a few deliberate beats, he was out,
His wings, a pale, dusted blue.

He began the slow discovery of
His immediate surroundings,
Taking in the sounds of the farmyard
And the general din of a household
Slowly stirring awake.

He wasn't one for frenzied exploration,
He watched me intently,
For the odd little organism that I was…
Flawed.

Wide- eyed.
A shade too silent.

His mute eyes conveyed discernment
As though he recognized me for who I was.
As though I had unwillingly let him in
On something inward.
It was perverse
How maddened I was.
I watched him,
As he flew past.

Crouching among shadows and sunbeams,
My hand, as though acting of its own accord,
Reached out and grasped him,
Crushed him to Finer than Dust.
I watched
As though from afar,
The shadow-play
Of his death,
Quick. Final.

My vision obscured,
I walked out
Into blindingness,
Longing to forget.

Learning

A mind, divided.
Without an anchor
To steady and sew his thoughts.

Thoughts, like the futile flurry of waves
In the depths of a conch.
His words, a rumbling echo
Of what was intended.

Divided at the tongue,
Receptacle and aperture,
Of thoughts still knotted up.

Belying himself, his nature,
He tried
Unraveling the knots,
Smoothing them down
Curing them with something foreign—
A language to be learned.

Up and out
Goes the tidal flurry,
Looming near
And then receding,
Constantly chipping away

A little more soil
In its fiery embrace.

Shadows and echoes
Battle in his mind.
The waves hit harder and faster now,
With steely purpose.
The knots come undone,
More soil chips away,
Gradually.

He straightens the knots out.
Lays them bare,
Examines them
With clinical detachment.

Words, no more a rumbling echo,
But louder and clearer in his head.
A mind, no longer divided,
But sewn together
In the new language of his thoughts.

He wades out,
His mind, sturdy and receptive
To the persistent tumult of waves, now
welcome—
A foreign tongue gradually yielding itself to his
command.

Legend

He surveyed the bloody expanse:

Platelets running fresh on silica,
Flesh and metal, borne into one.
Nature in despair,
A river pulsating with Less than Life,
Morbid-ity.

Legend, he was called,
Back home,
A far and distant place
Filling him with feelings that had no name.

The sour taste of death that passed him by,
That leveled the playing field of two opposing
forces...
The raw stench of fear beyond concealment.
The naked chill of Death,
Swift, self- sufficient, swooping.

Legend, he was called.
Beguiled
Into believing he was one,
He masqueraded
As one

With Might and Rage,
With the blood of warriors past
Coursing in his veins.

And yet,
Shivering, he stood
At the peak of what would
Become a glorious, landmark
Day in His story.
His-tory.
Apart from it,
A-part.

At the threshold of History,
He crouched, still wary
Of Death,
That old, cold friend
Of days, long and wintry,
Reeking of loss and other things unmentionable.

So,
The war cry that rose,
Not unbidden
In the hollow of his throat,
Escaped him,
A little defiantly,
But, the moment soon passed.

Legend, he was called

Upon returning.
His memory,
A defective, faulty thing,
Allowed him to forget the
Defiant war cry that
Betrayed his conscience.

Legend, he is called
To this day,
History books, having omitted
To record
His human moment.

Cycle Gap

Have you noticed
How effort and results
Are hardly ever proportional?

Take cycling for instance…
Pedal all you want,
But does it guarantee you speed?

What about all the times
You moved forward with little to no effort?
Perhaps it is the wind blowing in your favor,
Or your own strength while pedaling
From a few moments ago..

Perhaps..
This is your reminder
To embrace the pause,
Welcome uncertainty,
And focus some more
On the world running by you
And all its tiny miracles…

Who knows,
Your cycle could take you someplace new
Just let it…

A Whisper in the Waves

Just as a wave in retreat
Takes with it a piece of the shore,

It gifts us too, with
The golden warmth of
Sunlight, shattered,
A delightful tingle in our toes,
Glistening shells
That carried life not so long ago,
Planktons, invisible to the naked eye,
But there, nonetheless,

……..

We do not choose what hand
The universe deals us:
On this journey,
We will face trials and hardship,

Each wave,
A reminder to
Accept these with the same
Grace we showed,
When we were blessed with
Love, luck and joy.

Lighter

31

There is no journey
More uncomfortable than
Losing the weight of our ego
And unlearning our biases.

How little it takes to know that
We are already blessed,
And that today is most likely
Yesterday's prayer, answered.

In the short span of time we have left,
Let us become lighter travelers,
The only weight we carry, being
Gratitude and acts of kindness.

An Open Letter to Extroverts

Dear extroverts,

In a world that's built
To your convenience,
Where charisma and quick wit,
Small talk and repartee
Are rewarded,
Where climbing the 'social ladder'
Is a competitive sport, no less,

We exist too,
We who identify as introverts,
And no, it is not an affliction
That we suffer from,
Not to be confused with
Fear or reticence.

From time to time
We retreat from conversation
To an inner life
That's not devoid of color
As you may presume.
Our minds spin for us
As rich a tapestry
As you do, with social exchange.

You see,
Quietness can be powerful too,
And there is room enough
For the both of us.

On Healing

I hope you find the courage
To open your doors, once again,
To systems you judged,
Relationships you wrote off,
Places that elicited bad memories,
And mostly,
To yourself.

If you're one of the lucky ones,
You'll see how both
People and places
Hold the power to heal you,
When you let them.

Summer Vacation

35

Of long strolls in the park,
Grandad's promise of Dairy Milk,
Chasing your best friend under
Sunbeams and falling leaves,
Taking turns on the swing,

When everyday was a Sunday,
Spent daydreaming about
Becoming a grown up soon.

Blue Reverie

On a February morning in Havelock,
Beneath the sun's fiery gaze,
I stood, having minutes before,
Signed a liability waiver,
Entrusting myself in the hands
Of the scuba diver I just met.

Six of us, a motley gang,
Applied ourselves to
Learn just how to breathe and
Communicate twelve meters
Underneath the Indian Ocean.

Soon, our motorboat sped ahead,
Each wave we rode, bringing
Us closer to our dive site.
Silence fell upon us,
As the glittering turquoise waters
We first set eyes on,
Now engulfed us on all sides.
It was beauty and terror,
In equal measure.

Toppled underwater,
The unbearable weight

Of the scuba cylinder became
Insignificant underneath,
Much like our fears and anxieties
That have little actual bearing on reality,
And yet burden us.

Instinct made me wade in deeper now,
Fear gave in to curiosity,
My breathing quieted down
As the turquoise waters slowly
Darkened into a deeper blue,
Each step, away from sunlight.

Fish disguised as plants,
Bioluminescent plankton,
Plants with intricate trapping mechanisms
To keep away odd organisms
Like you and me,
Coral reefs and colorful fishes.

How could such a realm
Thrive just below sea level?
How could my fears of the ocean
Dissipate as they did?
Shortly after, our little expedition
Came to an end,
Flippers to feet again…

Sometimes, the trips we take

To the far corners of this world,
Bring us closer to who we are.
Savor each moment for what it is,
No matter what the next may bring,
Remember, no sadness or joy is absolute,
And the only pursuit worth having,
Is building a sanctuary for each other
To feel safe in.

And Yet...

I still remember the dream,
From not so long ago,
When I grappled with the voices in my head,

Arguments,
A clash of egos,
Hasty apologies,
And pleas to be understood,
Passed over,

When the entire world
Was brought to a grinding halt,
And I,
Locked in,
My mind, a dingy fortress,
Clouded by shadow and vapor,
Unbearably, split in two.

Each thought a sliver of who I once was,
Unreliable helmsmen who would
Keep me company
For the better part of a whole year.

A rag doll in limbo,
I oscillated between

Hope and misery,
Life and death.

How startingly simple it is,
To have your spirit broken,
To close off good reason,
Courage and softness
That once came to you
With little effort.

And yet…
Here I am,

Stirred from this dream,
Separated now by time,
People I met along the way,
Places that have now become a
Part of me,

Held and protected
By the ones I love,
Their voices, now offering me
The gifts of innocence, of hope.

And here comes the healing,
In starts and stops, at first
And then in waves,

I give in now

To a restful sleep,
Soon I will awake,
Knowing that life always finds a way
To set itself right again.

www.ingramcontent.com/pod-product-compliance
Lightning Source LLC
LaVergne TN
LVHW021308200726